Tragic Fires Throughout History ™

The Great Fire of London of 1666

Magdalena Alagna

rosen central ™

The Rosen Publishing Group, Inc., New York

Published in 2004 by The Rosen Publishing Group, Inc.
29 East 21st Street, New York, NY 10010

Library of Congress Cataloging-in-Publication Data

Alagna, Magdalena.
The Great Fire of London of 1666 / Magdalena Alagna.— 1st ed.
   p. cm. — (Tragic fires throughout history)
Summary: Recounts the events leading up to the 1666 fire that destroyed most
of London, tracing its course and aftermath, as well as the city's recovery.
Includes bibliographical references (p.) and index.
ISBN 0-8239-4485-9 (lib. bdg.)
1. Great Fire, London, England, 1666. 2. London (England)—History—17th
century. [1. Great Fire, London, England, 1666. 2. London (England)—
History—17th century.]
I. Title. II. Series.
DA681.A44 2004
942.1'2066—dc22

                                                          2003017307

Manufactured in the United States of America

CONTENTS

Introduction

In the year 1212, an enormous fire raged through the city of London, England, killing nearly 3,000 people and leaving much of the city in ruins. For more than four centuries, people called this fire the Great Fire—that was, until London experienced the fire that broke out on the morning of September 2, 1666.

Thomas Farynor, a baker for King Charles II, lived in a small house on Pudding Lane in central London. Farynor's house and shop were equipped with several ovens in which he and his assistant would bake goods for His Majesty. On the evening of September 1, 1666, Farynor went through his nightly routine, safely putting out the fires in each oven. But he forgot one.

Some burnt pieces of wood in the oven were still hot. They were hot enough to set fire to the stacks of fresh wood that were near the fireplace. Farynor's assistant woke a few hours later to find the house full of smoke. The house and the shop were ablaze! The assistant then woke the household, and they immediately searched for a way to escape the house. Farynor, his wife and daughter, and one assistant climbed to safety through an upstairs window. They traveled along the rooftops until they were safe from the fire. The maid was too scared to climb out the window and onto the roof.

The GREAT FIRE of LONDON in the Year 1666.

Printed soon after the Great Fire of 1666, this illustration depicts some of the destruction caused by the fire. St. Paul's Cathedral can be seen burning in the background. Eighty-seven churches were consumed by the blaze.

Because she stayed in the burning house, she would become the first casualty of the Great Fire of London.

London had a very dry summer that year, and the wooden buildings around the city acted like a well-stocked fireplace ready to burn. The fire quickly spread from Farynor's house and sparked the houses nearby. Strong winds carried the flames from building to building and block to block. The poorly constructed wooden buildings fed the inferno as it raced across the city. Within hours, the fire was out of control. The fire raged all through September 2 and 3. Unable to combat a fire of this size, London was paralyzed. In addition to the low water supplies, there was little firefighting equipment, and the city was poorly prepared. Londoners had little choice but to flee their city and watch it burn.

The fire lasted for five days and destroyed nearly 80 percent of the city. When the flames finally flickered out, the great city of London lay in ruins, a ghost of what it had been. A total of eighty-seven churches had been destroyed. Even the famous St. Paul's Cathedral had burned. The fire consumed 13,200 houses and left thousands of Londoners homeless. But in all this madness, only six people are definitely known to have died in the fire.

A tragedy of this size, which laid most of London to waste, could have destroyed a city forever. Ironically, the Great Fire was one of the events that eventually helped to improve London. The Great Fire burned up the small, crowded houses that were made of poor materials. With these houses gone, builders could make plans to construct better, safer houses, ones made of brick and stone instead of straw and wood. The fire also burned up a lot of the rats that were responsible for spreading the bubonic plague, a horrible disease that ravaged the entire country and most of Europe. The Great Fire helped the city in other ways, too. In its aftermath, people organized into what would become firefighting companies. Also, people wanted to make sure that they would be able to rebuild their lives, their businesses, and their fortunes after a natural disaster such as a big fire. This led to the creation of insurance companies. In the end, London would rise from its ashes to become the thriving metropolis it is today.

London Before the Great Fire

The Great Fire of London occurred during a period of England's history known as Stuart England (1603–1714), which was named after the royal family who ruled the country during that time. The first Stuart king was James I.

During seventeenth-century England, there was fighting between Roman Catholics and the followers of the Church of England, the Protestants. This conflict led to a plot to blow up the Houses of Parliament, where England's governing body meets. The Catholics wanted to kill King James I, who would be present for the opening of Parliament on November 5, 1605. Named the Gunpowder Plot, nearly thirty barrels of gunpowder were discovered hidden in a chamber beneath a Parliament building. Guy Fawkes, a Catholic sympathizer, was pinned as the mastermind behind the plot. He was tortured until he finally revealed others involved in the plot. Fawkes and several other people behind the Gunpowder Plot were soon executed. Today, Guy Fawkes Day is celebrated in England on November 5, complete with bonfires and fireworks, and Fawkes is burned in effigy.

During the Stuart reign, there were some wonderful changes made to beautify the city and enhance the quality of life for Londoners. One of those changes was the Covent Garden piazza. ("Piazza" is Italian for "square.") In 1631, Inigo Jones designed the Covent Garden piazza. It was the first square built in the city for the purpose of creating a space for residents to gather and to conduct trade. In 1637, Charles I opened Hyde Park to the public. Before that, only royalty could enjoy the beauties of Hyde Park. It was the first royal park to be made public.

James I, pictured here, narrowly escaped being assassinated by Roman Catholics who wanted to take control of Parliament.

Although the Stuarts ruled for more than a century, two major events in the years of 1665 and 1666 would define their reign: the bubonic plague and the Great Fire. While these two events would nearly destroy London—and ultimately lead to its rebuilding—the city and its people would have to survive them first.

The Bubonic Plague

In early 1665, the bubonic plague broke out in London. A plague is a disease that travels quickly from person to person

Many Londoners were dying from the plague in 1665. This illustration shows the horse-drawn carts that went around the city collecting corpses every morning. The horses were led by their drivers, who rang a bell and called out, "Bring out your dead!"

and brings with it great sickness and death. It was brought to London by rats aboard ships arriving from Holland in northwestern Europe. Some of these rats carried fleas infected with the plague. The plague had been in England since the Middle Ages, but the one that ravaged London in 1665 and 1666 was different. It was a plague so deadly and vicious that people could die just hours after infection. In the end, the plague claimed the lives of nearly 100,000 Londoners (out of the

400,000 or so who lived in the city). People all over London panicked, and many left for the sparsely populated country-side—even doctors and priests, who were needed to help treat the sick and care for the dying.

Londoners who had the plague were quarantined, or locked in their houses to prevent the disease from spreading. At first, people thought that dogs and cats spread the disease, so these animals were killed in masses. This was actually one of the worst things to do. Unknown to Londoners at the time, rats carrying plague-infected fleas spread the disease. Dogs and cats helped to keep the rat population from growing too large. By killing the cats and dogs, the rat population exploded, and the disease spread throughout the city. No one knew how the great plague could be stopped. The Great Fire of London would kill off much of the rat population and help stop the spread of the deadly disease.

Physicians wore birdlike masks during the plague outbreak. The "beak" of the mask contained herbs soaked in vinegar to mask the stench of the dead and dying. Some physicians thought the smell spread disease.

Living Conditions: Ready to Burn

In seventeenth-century London, most houses were made of wood and pitch, a sticky black material made from tar. Pitch is used to hold building materials together. It also acts as a coating to keep water from damaging the wood. The roofs of buildings were often thatched, or made of straw.

Fires in the city of London were not unusual. This was because not only were most buildings built from wood, but they were also heated and lit with open fires. In addition, houses were built close together. The city was very crowded, creating conditions where fire could easily jump from house to house and quickly get out of control.

In 1662, a law was passed that made every house shine a light between sunset and nine in the morning. The light was to help

Before the Great Fire, streets in London were lined with wooden buildings that had thatched roofs. Although less expensive to build than stone houses, these wooden structures became very flammable during the dry summer months. This is one of three known pictures of London before it was rebuilt—other drawings and prints were destroyed in the fire.

passersby see their way through the dark, crowded, and narrow streets. Today we have electric streetlights for this purpose. There was no such thing as electric streetlights in those days, so people used open flames to light the streets at night. Such lights might have helped people traveling at night, but they also increased the risk of fire in the city.

Fires and ways of dealing with fires were thought of differently in the seventeenth century. Fires were considered a local problem, meaning they were a problem only for those people living near the fire and not a problem for the whole city. Therefore, there was no organized fire company to serve all of London.

Up until the Great Fire of 1666, there were fairly simple ways of dealing with fire within the crowded city. If a fire broke out, buildings around it were pulled down to create a firebreak that

Although most of the city would be burned to the ground in 1666, London was rebuilt with stronger buildings and more organized streets. This map from 1572 shows how the city was laid out before the fire.

would stop the fire from spreading. Firebreaks helped because once a house was pulled down and debris was hauled away, a big pit of earth was created, where a fire could slow or stop completely. Besides the primitive tools used for firebreaks, there wasn't a lot of equipment on hand to deal with putting out fires once they had started. Each part of London had an official who was responsible for providing buckets and pumps for water and hooks for pulling down buildings. Outside of these practices, Londoners were not well prepared for emergencies.

London Is Burning

In the 1660s, London was the largest city in England, with a population of more than 400,000 people. (In Europe, only Paris was larger.) Fires were common in London during the seventeenth century. Houses were constructed from flammable material, and the city streets were narrow, so fire could travel quickly along them. At the same time, the narrow streets also meant that many fires could easily be stopped using fairly simple resources, such as buckets of water or firebreaks.

In April 1665, King Charles II warned the lord mayor of London, Sir Thomas Bludworth, of the danger caused by the narrow streets and wooden houses. In addition, a long, hot summer left London dry and caused a drought, leaving water reserves low. The city was ready to burn.

Many people believe the Great Fire of London started at Thomas Farynor's house. But no one knows for sure how it started. After the fire, Parliament organized a committee that looked into the cause of the fire. The committee asked Farynor what he knew about how the

At one time, the people of London were forced to pay a tax on every hearth, or fireplace, in their home. In this document, Thomas Farynor's hearths and ovens are counted for tax purposes. Farynor's ovens are the very ones believed to have sparked the Great Fire.

fire started. Farynor told the committee that he had gone through every room of his house before he went to sleep and that he had put out all the fires. In October 1666, an investigation into the fire was held at the Central Criminal Court of London, better known as Old Bailey. At the hearing, Farynor said that after midnight he had "gone through every room and found no fire, but in one chimney, where the room was paved with bricks, which fire I diligently raked up in embers . . . no window or door might let wind disturb them and that it was absolutely set on fire on purpose."

In the seventeenth century, houses were heated by fire so there were often several fireplaces in a house. According to the Old Bailey investigation, Farynor said that there was one fire that he didn't put out but "raked into embers." Embers are the remains of the fuel used for the fire and are hot enough to set fire to other things. Farynor believed that neither he nor his assistant was responsible for the fire. He claimed that someone had started the fire in his house on purpose. This was never proven.

Other people thought the fire started through the carelessness of the maid at the Farynor house. It was often the maid's job to put out the fires for the night before going to sleep. Some people thought that the maid did not put out the fires in the baker's great ovens. In January 1667, a Parliament committee officially declared the cause of the fire as "the hand of God, a great wind, and a very dry season." Today we would call that a natural disaster.

What we do know for sure is that Farynor's assistant woke at 2:00 AM to a house filled with smoke. The assistant then roused the Farynor family from sleep,

WILLIAM LILLY

William Lilly was known as the English Merlin. Merlin was a legendary magician and adviser to King Arthur. William Lilly had supposedly predicted the Great Fire fourteen years before it actually happened. Some people thought Lilly might have started the fire himself so that his prediction would come true. Then he would be seen as a great prophet. On October 25, 1666, Lilly was ordered to appear before a special committee set up to learn the cause of the Great Fire. Lilly was able to convince the committee that he had nothing to do with the Great Fire.

and they escaped the burning house by climbing onto the roof and traveling by rooftop to safety.

Sparking the Fire

Sparks from Farynor's burning house fell on hay and straw in the next-door yard of the Star Inn at Fish Street Hill. It was a windy morning, so the sparks spread quickly, carried on the wind. As the sparks fell, they set fire to the straw roofs and wooden buildings nearby. In the early-morning hours of September 2, Lord Mayor Bludworth was informed of the fire, but he was not too worried about it. After all, fires often happened in London, and they were just as often put out without any major problems. The mayor was worried about prematurely pulling down houses to make firebreaks. At that time, there was no insurance to provide money to rebuild the houses once they were torn down. As the mayor dismissed the fire, the blaze grew with every passing minute. Bludworth's hesitation at taking action would allow the fire time to get out of control. The mayor did not know then that this would be a fire unlike any that London had ever seen.

The Fire Breaks Out

From the Star Inn, the fire burned St. Margaret's Church and then entered Thames Street. Thames Street had many warehouses, each filled with products such as oil, alcohol, straw, coal, and tallow

The Thames was the safest place to wait out the fire. People piled into boats on the river, hoping to escape the blaze. The waterway soon became clogged with boats.

(used to make candles). All of these products are highly flammable, and they fed the fire that would consume London. Soon, the fire became so strong that it could not be put out with the buckets of water and the hand pumps that were typically used.

By mid-morning, just hours after the fire started, the flames were halfway across London Bridge. The design of London Bridge consisted of two groups of buildings separated by a large open space. That space had acted as a firebreak during a fire in 1632. It did the same thing this time. Fortunately, only one-third of the magnificent bridge was burned.

Diarist Samuel Pepys lived nearby, and on Sunday morning he walked to the Tower of London. There he saw the fire heading west, pushed onward by the strong winds. Pepys wrote, "I walked to the Tower . . . and there I did see the houses at the end of the bridge all on fire . . . nobody in my sight endeavoring to quench it, but to remove their goods and leave all to the fire."

Many people tried to flee the burning city by boat, causing chaos on the river Thames, the city's main waterway. Mayor

Samuel Pepys *(left)* and John Evelyn *(right)* were both writers who witnessed the fire. Theirs are among the best firsthand accounts of the disaster available to us today.

Bludworth did not know what to do to stop the fire. He thought that the ordinary methods of buckets and hand pumps would work.

As Pepys watched the fire from the Tower of London, he saw how strong the fire was growing and knew that action needed to be taken—and quickly! Pepys worked for the king, so he could get a private audience with His Majesty. Pepys went to King Charles II and the king's brother, James, the Duke of York. Pepys told them about the fire and how it could destroy the city. The king ordered that houses be pulled down to create firebreaks. It was done, but the fire did not stop. By the time the houses had been pulled down, the rubble from the houses just became fuel for the fire. It seemed that nothing they could do would slow the inferno.

The wind continued to whip through London and spread the fire at an alarming rate. The fire moved with such ferocity it could jump firebreaks that were twenty houses long. By evening, the fire was so strong that it continued to spread wildly—even against the wind. The fire headed toward the Tower of London, the grand building that, over the years, had been used as a prison, an armory, and storage for the crown jewels.

By evening the scene was a nightmare. From the banks of the Thames, Pepys described the fire as "one entire arch of fire from this to the other side of the bridge and in a bow up the hill, for an arch above a mile long." Fellow writer and diarist John Evelyn recalled the nighttime sky as "light as day for 10 miles around." It seemed as though the city would be gone by morning.

September 3, 1666: The Height of the Inferno

By the early morning of September 3, the fire was raging north and west through London. A thick cloud of black smoke hung over the city, making it hard for people to see the sun. When they did see the sun, it hung red like a ball of fire in the sky. Even miles away from London, the sky glowed red. The fire was so huge it created a strong wind that blew debris into the air, making it hard for people to breathe. Soon people began to panic. When King Charles II woke in Whitehall Palace that day, he received bad news about the fire from a messenger: An important steel yard on the riverbank had burned. Additionally, Boar's Head Tavern, a landmark where playwright William Shakespeare used to visit, was gone.

King Charles II decided that he was going to take control of the situation. The fire was so bad that he could no longer leave the firefighting to the independent local officials scattered throughout the city. The king asked his brother, the Duke of York, for help and made him his deputy, or an official who helps to organize people to carry out the king's orders. The Duke of York organized efforts to stop the fire by setting up a system of defense against the inferno. The defense consisted of groups of people, called fire posts, set up at the edges of the fire in different places around the city. These groups were made up of ordinary Londoners, as well as soldiers, a police officer, and a few noblemen. The noblemen would report to the Duke of York on the progress of the fire.

Although King Charles II did his best to organize people to fight the fire, no amount of effort was able to stop it.

The Duke of York also organized militias from counties near London to help fight the fire. Militias are groups of ordinary citizens who have some training in how to work together as a team, usually against some kind of threat such as war. The militias also helped stop people from looting, or taking advantage of the chaos to steal goods from businesses or homes whose owners were running for their lives. Some accounts of the fire noted that people hired carts and drivers to carry their goods and furniture out of the city. Sometimes a driver would take a family's goods and drive off, and the family never saw their belongings again!

People didn't have time to pack up their possessions as the fire spread, so they quickly grabbed what they could and ran. Despite the panicked exodus from the city, only six people were confirmed to have died in the fire.

A Desperate Fight

The flames then ate up Gracechurch Street, where the fruit and herb markets were located. Lombard Street, a major financial center, was also in danger. People gathered in the streets to watch the work of the houses being pulled down. Soldiers and police officers on horses were stationed at the edges of the crowd to make sure people did not get hurt. By mid-afternoon on September 3, the smoke could be seen from Oxford, a town nearly sixty miles (96 kilometers) from London.

The fire posts worked heroically to battle the fire, but there were serious water shortages that hurt their chances of success.

The water system for the city was a series of wooden pipes that pumped water from the Thames and the New River. There were places in the pipes that were designed to let water out. However, because the pipes were made of wood, it was easy to cut through them and get water. During the panic, that's exactly what many Londoners did to douse the flames. Because there were so many cuts in the pipe, water only trickled out and the water pipes were useless in helping fight the fire.

The streets were filled with citizens trying to escape the burning city. Londoners had begun to run to the open spaces of Moorsfield and Finsbury Hill. Although some people took advantage of the chaos to loot the city, there were many more people who helped each other and tried to save their city. Priests saved the wealth in the churches. Students

PINNING THE BLAME ON SOMEONE

The Great Fire was such a tragedy that some people tried to explain it by placing blame in strange places. For instance, many people blamed Catholics for starting the fire. There was a strong feeling against Catholics in London at that time, because the official church was not the Catholic Church but the Church of England. Additionally, Britain was at war with France, Spain, Holland, and Ireland, so many people thought that people from these countries could have started the Great Fire. Unfortunately, some people from those countries who were in London at the time had their property stolen or their houses vandalized.

Leather buckets such as this one *(top)* were ineffective in combating the fire and were replaced by hoses in later years. Water pipes *(bottom)* were made out of wood, and firefighters would drill holes in the pipes when they needed water to fight a fire.

in the school at Westminster poured buckets of water on the church, St. Dunstan-in-the-East, a magnificent building boasting the second highest church steeple in London.

Just as it seemed the fire was finally contained, it jumped over the firebreak at Mercers' Hall and began to burn up Cheapside, a wealthy street in London. The work of pulling down houses to make firebreaks was not going fast enough with the tools that were available. Finally, officials decided to blow up the houses with gunpowder so that they would fall faster. Pepys wrote in his diary, "Blowing up houses . . . stopped the fire when it was done, bringing down the houses in the same places they stood, and then it was easy to quench what little fire was in it."

"All the sky was of a fiery aspect, like the top of a burning oven, and the light seen above 40 miles round about . . . 10,000 houses all in one flame, the noise and cracking and thunder of the impetuous flames, the shrieking of women and children . . . London was, but is no more!"
—John Evelyn, describing the scene on September 3, 1666

By the evening of September 3, the inferno had reached its peak. Again, the city was lit up in flames that raged through the night. The fire was moving in two places, in the west near the river Thames and in the north. The two paths of the fire met at Stocks Market. Hundreds of houses had fallen, and thousands of Londoners were left homeless, forced to take refuge in the fields at Moorsfield and Finsbury Hill.

4

September 4, 1666: The Beginning of the End

The fire continued to grow during the night, and on the morning of September 4, King Charles II learned that Cheapside was burning. Cheapside was a major financial center as well as one of the most historic streets in London, having survived from the Middle Ages. The houses and shops on this street were some of the most beautiful in the entire city. On September 4, King Charles II rode through the city, tossing gold coins to the firefighters to reward them for their hard work. Not only did King Charles II and the Duke of York ride around on horseback overseeing things, but they also pitched in and worked alongside the commoners to help fight the inferno.

After burning up Cheapside, the fire went on to Guildhall, where the city's records were kept. Some of these records dated back to the thirteenth century. There was no way that the records could be removed in time—they were too heavy and there were too many of them. The fire did burn up Guildhall, but the records were stored in the basement of the building, which was lined with stone walls, and miraculously, the records did not burn!

The fire went two different ways from Guildhall. It went west to Aldersgate, which was a stone tower built into the city wall. All day the fire licked at the tower's gate, and by afternoon the fire burst through the gate, burned up about thirty houses beyond it, and then stopped. North from Guildhall, the fire moved toward Coopers' Hall. Coopers are craftsmen who make barrels. Many craftsmen met in groups called guilds, which had special places for their meetings, such as Coopers' Hall. The fire burnt up Coopers' Hall and then moved north to Cripplegate, one of the city's gates where sick people who couldn't work begged for money. It was there that workers in the fire posts began using gunpowder to blow up buildings.

People grew afraid after hearing the explosions of the gunpowder. They thought that perhaps the city was under attack. This only added to the panic that now had a stranglehold on the city. It was becoming impossible to find a cart and a driver willing to leave London. Drivers were asking extremely high sums of money to carry people's goods out of the city. Many people fled on foot. Sick people were carried in their beds through the streets. Some people fainted at the side of the road.

St. Paul's Cathedral

Although demolition, or blowing up houses, began to take effect in the east, the fire was still traveling along Fleet Street toward Chancery Lane in the west. Flames soon surrounded St Paul's

Cathedral, one of the most magnificent buildings in England. Constructed in the eleventh century, the cathedral was under repair and covered in scaffolding, or wood on which workers could walk to fix parts of the building. Additionally, the smoke from the burning coal used to provide heat had weakened the stone walls of the cathedral. On the evening of September 4, 1666, St. Paul's Cathedral started to burn, ignited by the scaffolding. The thousands of books stored in the cathedral only added fuel to the fire. The roof beams in the ceiling of the cathedral were made of timber, so they also

St. Paul's Cathedral was burned in the Great Fire, attacked by Vikings, struck by lightning, used as a marketplace, and damaged by artillery fire during the English Civil Wars. It has been rebuilt several times.

burned quickly. The lead roof melted, and stones exploded from the heat. King Charles II and the Duke of York rode on horseback as close as they dared and watched, astonished, as the sides of the building caved in, revealing a pit of flames inside the beloved cathedral.

"The stones of St. Paul's flew like grenados [grenades], the melting lead running down the streets in a stream and the very pavements glowing with fiery redness, so as no horse nor man was able to tread on them."
—John Evelyn, describing the scene as the great church collapsed

While St. Paul's burned in the early morning of September 5, the fire continued its path of destruction as it burned up Bridewell Prison. Some of the city's massive stores of grain were stored in the prison, and the fire burned these, too. The fire was so hot that the dead burned in the graveyards. By nighttime, the fire was almost at the Tower of London. Usually, a massive amount of gunpowder was stored in the tower, and if it caught fire, the explosion could blow up nearby London Bridge. The tower was also where the crown jewels were kept. Luckily both the gunpowder and the crown jewels had been moved to a safer place earlier that day. The jewels had been moved to Whitehall Palace, where the king and queen lived.

Near midnight on September 4, the wind died down. The fire's rampage began to slow, yet the fire would continue for days. The people who were camped out in Moorsfield started to set up markets so that transplanted Londoners could still eat and keep up

Early fire extinguishers looked like large metal syringes. They were not very effective when used against large fires. The lithograph *(above)* shows this type of fire extinguisher being put to use during a large fire in London.

their strength to fight the fire. There were a few outbreaks of fire on September 5, 1666, but by nighttime the fire was under control.

The Damage

By September 6, the Great Fire of London was all but over. The fire would smolder for a few more days and reveal a terrible aftermath. In the end, the Great Fire of 1666 burned 80 percent of London, from Fleet Street in the west to the Tower of London in the east. The fire had raged from the north to the banks of the river Thames all the way south to the wall at Cripplegate. Within the area of the fire, no building survived in one piece aboveground. The damage included 13,200 houses, 87 churches (including St. Paul's Cathedral), Castle Baynard at Blackfriars, Bridewell Prison, Newgate Prison, Guildhall, three city gates, the Custom House, four stone bridges, the Royal Exchange, and 52 company halls. The city lay in ruins.

"The poor inhabitants were dispersed about St. George's Fields, and Moorsfield, as far as Highgate, and several miles in circle, some under tents, some under miserable huts and hovels, many without a rag or any necessary utensils, bed or board, who from delicateness, riches, and easy accommodations in stately and well furnished houses, were now reduced to extremest misery and poverty."
—John Evelyn, describing the scene at Moorsfield

This map of London shows the extent of damage caused by the Great Fire. The white area is the part of the city ravaged by the inferno.

Now the city had to rebuild. But there was so much to do, it was difficult to know where to start. However, there was one immediate concern: tens of thousands of homeless Londoners were camped in Moorsfield. The first thing King Charles II did was to restore the control of the city to the city officials. Then he made available food for the homeless as well as wood so that people could start to rebuild their homes and businesses.

The Rebuilding of London

The Great Fire had proved to Londoners that the city needed a more efficient way to deal with fires. Gone were the days when buckets for water and primitive tools for firebreaks were the only equipment necessary.

The Great Fire also provided an opportunity to build an entirely new city. London after the fire was a very different place from the city that had existed before. Londoners had wanted to remodel their city for years. Now was their chance. The Great Fire helped to make London into a more modern city. However, it wasn't possible to redesign the entire city from scratch. People whose property had been burned in the fire still wanted to keep their ownership of the land. That meant the city officials couldn't just build whatever they wanted to, wherever they wanted it. They had to work with the citizens.

Several changes did take place. Streets were made broader, and they were placed more evenly apart instead of crowded together. Also, buildings were made of brick and stone instead of wood and straw. Regulations were set up to make sure that buildings would be uniform, or the same, depending on where the buildings were located in the city. Two-story buildings went on the small streets. Three-story buildings went on the larger streets and on the streets by the river. Four-story buildings could only be built on the city's largest and most important streets.

The Organization of Fire Companies and Fire Insurance

After the Great Fire, many people had nothing left. Their homes and their possessions had all been destroyed in the fire. Although a large fire can be terrible for many people today, most people have fire insurance to help replace material possessions that can be destroyed in a fire. People did not have fire insurance in 1666. Soon after the Great Fire, people in the city recognized the need for fire insurance.

Insurance plates, such as this one, indicated which company provided a building with its fire coverage.

The way an insurance policy works is that a homeowner gives small amounts of money to the insurance company on a regular basis. If disaster strikes, such as a fire burning down a house, the homeowner can get money from the insurance company to rebuild the house. After the Great Fire, insurance companies began to spring up. Charters, or money from the government, were granted and allowed the insurance industry to flourish.

Soon the insurance companies realized that with more efficient firefighting, they would not have to pay so much to property owners with damaged property. The insurance companies decided to hire people to put out fires. The companies got new fire engines with better firefighting equipment, and they hired men who would be specially trained to fight fires. Soon firefighting companies were formed.

"I did within these six days see smoke still remaining of the late fire in the City; and it is strange to think how to this very day I cannot sleep a-night without great terrors of fire; and this very night I could not sleep till almost 2 in the morning through thoughts of fire."
—Samuel Pepys, February 17, 1667, more than four months after the Great Fire

In the beginning, the insurance companies set up a system to make sure that their firefighters put out fire only in the houses that were insured by the insurance company. Each person who had insurance was given a metal plate to hang outside of the house. When a fire broke out, firefighters from different insurance companies rushed to the scene to see which insurance company's plate was on the building. If the building did not carry their mark, they would leave. They even let buildings burn down!

The insurance industry expanded throughout the eighteenth century. In 1833, the Sun Insurance Company and ten other

The most important architect behind London's reconstruction was Sir Christopher Wren *(inset)*. He designed dozens of new buildings, including fifty-two churches. His plans to rebuild the streets, pictured here, were initially rejected but eventually accepted by city officials.

companies set up the first single firefighting force to cover the entire city of London.

Christopher Wren, Famous Architect

On September 10, 1666, the great architect Christopher Wren approached King Charles II with a plan to rebuild the city. Wren began his career as a scientist and was a professor of astronomy at Oxford University from 1661 to 1673. After deciding to devote his career to architecture, Wren got his first architect's job with the help of his uncle, who was a bishop. Wren's first job was to redesign Pembroke College Chapel at Cambridge University, which was completed in 1665. Next he designed the Sheldonian Theatre in Oxford, completed in 1669. It was based on the Roman Theatre of Marcellus and would become the work that made Wren famous as an architect.

After the Great Fire, Wren submitted plans for the rebuilding of London. His initial plans were turned down. He then focused his design efforts on London's churches. In the end, his plans won over city officials. Wren eventually designed fifty-two churches, including the new St. Paul's Cathedral.

CHRISTOPHER WREN

Christopher Wren died at the age of ninety and was buried in St. Paul's Cathedral. No monument was put on his grave at the time. His epitaph, or the words Wren wanted put on his grave, was carved in Latin over one of the great doors of the cathedral: *Lector, si monumentum requiris, circumspice*—"Reader, if it is a monument you seek, look about you."

The Monument

Wren also made plans for a monument to stand as remembrance of the Great Fire. The memorial, simply called the Monument,

Wren's Monument stands as a constant reminder to the people of London that their city was able to survive the ravages of the Great Fire.

took six years to complete (1671–1677) and stands in a small square open to the public. The street on which it was built was called Fish Street but was renamed Monument Street. The Monument is a 202-foot-tall (61.6-meter) stone column. The base of the monument, on which the pedestal rests, is 28 square feet (2.6 square meters). Inside the Monument is a black marble staircase, containing 345 steps that lead to a balcony at the top of the Monument. The north and south sides of the pedestal each have a Latin inscription. One inscription describes the city immediately after the fire—how London looked like a city made of ashes. The other inscription describes the city's glorious rebirth. More than 300 years later, Christopher Wren's Monument still stands at the center of London, a testament to the perseverance and determination of a great city and its people.

Timeline

Saturday, September 1, 1666

9 PM

Thomas Farynor, the king's baker, puts out his ovens and goes to bed. One fire is left smoldering.

Sunday, September 2, 1666

1–2 AM

The household is awakened by Farynor's assistant. The house is on fire as Farynor, his family, and one assistant escape.

3 AM

The fire consumes Farynor's house and shop. The fire then sparks nearby buildings, including the Star Inn on Fish Street Hill.

4 AM

Lord Mayor Sir Thomas Bludworth is informed of the fire. He dismisses it.

5 AM

The fire reaches Thames Street and warehouses filled with flammable materials.

8 AM

The fire is halfway across London Bridge.

10 AM

Samuel Pepys goes to Whitehall to inform the king that drastic action must be taken.

7 PM

Londoners begin to evacuate the city, fleeing to Moorsfield and Finsbury Hill.

Monday, September 3, 1666

9 AM

The Duke of York is put in charge of a centralized firefighting operation.

41

5 PM

Officials decide to blow up houses using gunpowder to create firebreaks.

7 PM

The fire rapidly moves east and destroys Billingsgate.

Tuesday, September 4, 1666

8 AM

The fire reaches its peak, ten times larger that it was on Sunday night.

Late Morning

The fire reaches Cheapside, the city's market.

3 PM

Buildings around the Tower of London are blown up with gunpowder, saving the tower.

8 PM

The fire reaches St. Paul's Cathedral.

9 PM

The fire splits into two directions. Coopers' Hall is destroyed. The fire moves north toward Cripplegate.

Wednesday, September 5, 1666

1 AM

The fire consumes St. Paul's Cathedral.

3 AM

Bridewell Prison is destroyed.

9 AM

Finally, the winds die down. The fire is soon under control.

Noon

Cripplegate is saved, "where the King himself was seen helping the soldiers," according to Samuel Pepys.

Thursday, September 6, 1666

Noon

The fire is out except for a few small blazes. The Great Fire has destroyed most of the city, including 87 churches, 52 livery halls, and 13,200 houses. Miraculously, only six people died.

Glossary

catastrophe (kuh-TAS-truh-fee) An event that causes much harm.

cathedral (kuh-THEE-druhl) A large church run by a bishop.

chaos (KAY-ahs) Complete lack of order.

debris (duh-BREE) The remains of something broken down or destroyed.

efficient (ih-FIH-shent) Done in the best way possible.

effigy (EH-fuh-jee) A figure that represents a person.

execute (EK-suh-kyoot) To be put to death.

exodus (EK-so-duss) A mass departure.

flammable (FLA-muh-bul) Capable of being lit on fire and burning quickly.

impetuous (im-PETCH-wus) Marked by violent force or movement.

inferno (in-FER-noh) A huge fire.

Middle Ages (MIH-dul AY-jez) The period in European history from about AD 500 to about 1450.

monument (MON-yoo-ment) Something that is built to remember or give honor to a person or an event.

reign (RAYN) The time in which one rules.

smolder (SMOHL-der) To burn with a low heat.

London Fire Brigade Museum
Winchester House
94A Southwark Bridge Road
London, SE1 0EG
England
Web site: http://www.london-fire.gov.uk/about_us/our_history/visit_
   our_museum.asp

Museum of London
London Wall
London EC2Y 5HN
England
Web site: http://www.museum-london.org.uk

Web Sites

Due to the changing nature of Internet links, the Rosen Publishing Group, Inc., has developed an online list of Web sites related to the subject of this book. This site is updated regularly. Please use this link to access the list:

http://www.rosenlinks.com/tfth/gfls

For Further Reading

Bell, Walter G. *The Great Fire of London in 1666*. Westport, CT: Greenwood Publishing Group, 1971.

Clout, Hugh, ed. *The Times History of London*. London: Times Books, 1999.

Ellis, Peter Berresford. *The Great Fire of London: An Illustrated Account*. London: New English Library, 1986.

Lang, Jane. *Rebuilding St. Paul's After the Great Fire of London*. Oxford, England: Oxford University Press, 1956.

Porter, Stephen. *The Great Fire of London*. Gloucestershire, England: Sutton Publishing 1996.

Schofield, John. *The Building of London: From the Conquest to the Great Fire*. London: British Museum, 1984.

Weiss, David A. *The Great Fire of London*. Illustrated by Joseph Papin. New York: Crown Publishers, 1968.

Bibliography

Anglia Campus. "London Fire: The Great Fire of London—1666."
    Retrieved February 2003 (http://www.angliacampus.com/
    education/fire/london/history/greatfir.htm).

BBCi. "London After the Great Fire." Retrieved February 2003
    (http://www.bbc.co.uk/history/society_culture/society/
    after_fire_01.shtml).

History Learning Site."The Great Fire of London of 1666."
    Retrieved February 2003 (http://www.historylearningsite.co.uk/
    great_fire_of_london_of_1666.htm).

London Ancestor. "The Monument." Retrieved February 2003
    (http://www.londonancestor.com/leighs/pb-monum.htm).

Luminarium. "The Great Fire of London, 1666." Retrieved
    February 2003 (http://www.luminarium.org/encyclopedia/
    greatfire.htm).

Pepys, Samuel. *The Diary of Samuel Pepys: A New and Complete
    Transcription*. Edited by Robert Latham and William Matthews.
    London: HarperCollins, 1995.

Weiss, David A. *The Great Fire of London*. Illustrated by Joseph
    Papin. New York: Crown Publishers, 1968.

Index

About the Author

Magdalena Alagna is an editor and freelance writer living and working in New York City.

Photo Credits

Cover, pp. 1, 10 Private Collection/Bridgeman Art Library; p. 5 The Art Archive/Private Collection/Eileen Tweedy; p. 9 Roy Miles Fine Paintings/ Bridgeman Art Library; p. 11 Bibliothèque Nationale, Paris, France/ Archives Charmet/Bridgeman Art Library; p. 12–13 from *Histoire de L'entrée de la Reine Mere dans la Grande Bretagne*, by P. de la Serre; p. 14 Glasgow University Library, Scotland/Bridgeman Art Library; p. 16 The National Archive, UK; pp. 19, 24 © Hulton/Archive/Getty Images; p. 20 (left) Royal Society of Arts, London, UK/Bridgeman Art Library; p. 20 (right) Philip Mould, Historical Portraits Ltd, London, UK/Bridgeman Art Library; p. 23 Private Collection/Philip Mould, Historical Portraits Ltd, London, UK/ Bridgeman Art Library; p. 26 (top) The Art Archive/London Museum/Eileen Tweedy; pp. 26 (bottom), 36 courtesy of the New York City Fire Museum; pp. 30, 34, 38 Guildhall Library, Corporation of London; p. 32 (top) © Historical Picture Archive/Corbis; p. 32 (bottom) © Museum of London; p. 38 (inset) Royal Hospital Chelsea, London, UK/Bridgeman Art Library; p. 40 The Art Archive/John Webb.

Designer: Les Kanturek; Editor: Charles Hofer;
Photo Researcher: Amy Feinberg